# SEARCHING FOR FREEDOM

## *KATIE GRADEN SPENCE*

K Graden Spence xx

To Sharon and John,
thank you so much for all your support!
Love Katie xo

ISBN: 9781731345745

Cover Design by Annie Louise Twitchell

Cover Image by Stephen Ferguson

Proofreading by Mr. McMillan and Dr. Hewitt

*Dedicated to Thriving Life Church.*

# Acknowledgements

There are far too many people to acknowledge you all individually, but to my family, friends, teachers, and my incredible church, I want to say a massive thank you for your continued encouragement, inspiration and support. Each and every one of you have contributed positively to my journey, and in turn, helped to create this poetry anthology about my personal story of finding God and battling mental illness. Also, a massive shout-out to Annie Louise Twitchell for designing my anthology cover, to Stephen Ferguson for taking this awesome photograph for my book and to Mr. McMillan and Dr Hewitt for completing a proof read of my anthology.

**Flight Mode**

I want to get away,
Fly away.
To the French Caribbean or Berlin City.
Where the sun shines,
And your life is as bright as you can make it.
Away from these exams;
That cause me stress.
Away from the people,
Who never want me to succeed.
Away away,
I just want to fly away.
I want to travel by trains
Faster than the speed of sound,
So I don't have to feel this pain anymore.
Maybe then my anxiety would fade,
If only, if only.
Maybe then I could relax,
Instead of my heart racing faster
Than a formula one racing car.
Maybe then I would have the confidence
For my dreams to come true,
Instead of sitting here lonely in a chair
Shaking like a wet dog at the most horrific thoughts.
Say goodbye to the streets of Newtownards,
Where the troubles of my childhood follow me.
See the world in a different light,
And new cities that fulfil my destiny.
Take me to flight mode, away from this harsh reality.
Take me to paradise, I don't want to live this life anymore.

## Bursting Bubbles

Lost within myself,
My own feelings battering me inside,
The world as chaotic as ever,
And my own tipped upside down.
Trapped and alone,
Yet in the company of everyone I know.
Standing having a conversation,
Yet occupied by my own troubling thoughts,
With no focus or realisation
Of what's going on
Even a few steps in front
Or a few steps behind.
Not many people have noticed,
That I have become more distant,
Because I hide it so well,
With a beaming smile
That disguises what I certainly cannot hide at home.
Everyday has become a hurdle,
That I no longer even want to face
Because I am still waiting to be saved by grace.
Why can't these people see
How everything has suddenly changed in me?
That I am being swallowed by sink holes inside,
Desperate to reach out
Because I can no longer hide the trauma in me.
Afraid to speak up,
And too anxious to sit down.
Trapped in this cycle
That is drowning me inside;
Gobbled by the ocean,
And strangled by the snakes;
Slashed with a knife,
And torn apart by the hungry lions
Because this is what it feels like in my soul

As each emotion collides,
And I long for that day
When the bubbles will burst,
And I will hopefully come alive.

Please Lord, I cannot cope,
I have no foundation, salvation of destination,
Just questions with no answers,
And an unfulfilled purpose.
I cannot do this alone,
Come and rescue me,
Call me out into all that I can be.

As afternoon approached,
And the school day was coming to an end,
Death was arrested,
And my life began!

**Can you hear me?**

Doubt strangles you dangerously inside,
Suddenly your heart is ripped apart,
Your brain is poisoned,
And even your blood is lacking positivity.
Confidence is no longer your best friend,
And before you know it
The devil has a frightening foothold.
Your strength almost becomes invisible,
And your weaknesses, well,
They give you an almighty smack.
You may still believe in others
Meanwhile your own self esteem
Is suffering silently.
You're drowning miserably on the inside,
Yet strangely still smiling on the outside.

Sometimes not many people know;
Maybe only those you barely even speak to.
Even your family and friends can't cure it
Because it's something only you can overcome.

Your hobbies become someone else's
As you lose interest in everything you love.

'Just get on with it!' society yells;
'Just stop trying!' depression screams;
'Just give up now!' the devil commands.


The Lord yells 'stop listening immediately,'
But for a moment His voice is distant,
And you can only see the constant mayhem.

Then miraculously He drowns your heart,
But this time in unfailing love.
He fills your brain,
But this time with His encouraging words.
He boosts your blood,
But this time with esteem and confidence.

Even when your heart is peeling,
He can still perform tremendous healing.
Only He can ever beat the devil,
For the Lord has overcome the world.

As morning approaches,
And the street lights fade,
You must remember His light,
And how it never drops a shade.
As night approaches,
And the world becomes much quieter,
You must remember His word,
And how it can only shout louder.
I was drowning,
But now I'm not even frowning.
My doubt sparked a fighter in me-
I see my life beyond the hiccups and cracks,
I see my mistakes as simply a work in progress.
The storm sailed me to my security,
And the hurricanes hurled the power of Jesus at me.
Breaking point to turning point,
Breakdown to breakthrough.
What ever happened to the old Katie that I once knew?
I don't see or feel her often now:
Maybe her ship sailed,
Maybe she got cold feet,
But the warrior has emerged,
And the worrier has fled.
Barriers have come crashing down

As fears have been demolished,
And hope has soared through my life.
I have faded and shone again
Because I live in the now and not then.

I leave you with these words
To help fix your brokenness.
As you take the leaps and bounds,
I promise your Father will heal the wounds.
Stand with the world behind you,
And let the devil know he has no hope.
Stand for Christ alone, your King,
And don't ever give the devil any scope.

Breathe and believe,
Pick yourself up,
And when the world says give up,
Please promise me you won't.

**I am Young**

Oh, I will sing my song
Like I am unafraid;
Oh, I will sing my song
For the world to hear.

And I will run, I will fight.
The trouble won't get to me.
I will change the world,
Oh yeah, you will see.

I am young,
I am young,
But that won't stop me.

Oh, the beat
Beneath my feet
Is changing me,
And my life transformed for all to see.

I will rise,
I will rise,
Like I am new.

Oh, the cave
Won't haunt me;
The dark won't frighten me
For I have been set free.
My heart is bursting
With passion and fire.

I will shine,
I will shine,
Like I am on my way.

## I know

I know your stomach is sick right now,
And I know you think it would be easier to just give up.
I know your heart is racing faster than ever,
And I know you think it won't slow its' pace.
I know your legs are trembling,
And I know you think others are staring.
I know you are blinded at the moment,
And I know you think the fog will never clear.
I know you are walking on troubled waters,
And I know you think that within moments, you will sink.
I know you are struggling just to survive,
And I know you are wondering whether you will ever thrive.
Life is sucking you in and you don't know whether to run or hide-
You don't know what is happening,
You don't know when it started,
You don't know when it is going to end;
You don't even know if it will come to a halt.
All you know is that it's horrific inside,
And there is simply no way for you to describe.
Anchors rip your drive down,
Brakes steal your speed,
Enemies replace your positive voice,
And you just can't listen right now.
Words ring through your head,
Yet silence is an eerie and uncomfortable presence.
Freedom, what is that?
Music that used to satisfy your soul,
Now sends shivers through your body,
It traps you in your own unwanted thoughts,
And forces you to hit stop.
You're alive, yet you feel absolutely nothing,
And if you're really honest, you don't want to feel something
Because anything you feel is suffering.

Anything you hear is frightening,
Anything you speak is consumed with anxiety,
Anything you touch seems to slip away before you,
Anything you see is a blur because your vision is non-existent.

But at the rear of your mind, something is keeping you going,
A spark is still lit when everything else is dull.
There is an entrance to your cave, you came through it, didn't you?
Let your footsteps retrace your path,
Let bricks of that self-built wall come crashing down,
Let bridges be constructed to lead you;
Let the troubles in your life become someone else's light source.

Do not worry about tomorrow for tomorrow will worry about itself,
Dear Friend, remember each day has enough trouble of its own.

## No More

Hey devil get out of my mind,
Don't you see that you can't make God blind?
You think I'm your child,
But don't you see that God is my Father?
I won't ever let you trouble me,
God will call me out into all I can be.
You need to go away
Because you won't pull me astray.
He will forever lead me
Away from the temptations
You bring to me.
You tell me I'm not enough,
Well guess what?
God is making me tough!
And that my friend is 100% fact!
Stop playing childish games with me,
I know God's definitely healing me.
All you send through the post is hate and fear,
But my God doesn't even make me shed a tear.
He fills my soul with peace and joy,
While you treat me like a dog's least favourite toy.

You think I can't see what you're doing,
But you forget God knows where I'm going.
He has a plan for me,
Not like you
Who only loses me.

## Hidden Letters in Envelopes

I wonder if someone asked you to open the envelopes of your mind,
The ones you've locked firmly in your filing cabinet,
Tell me, what would the letters read inside?
The smile you're showing everyone around you,
Or the frown clouding your inner and hidden face.
The laughter you're echoing through the halls,
Or the 'HELP ME!' you want to scream.
The 'yes, I'm great' and 'how's you?' stance,
Or, 'I'm really flipping rubbish, but where do I even begin?'
The musical harmonisation throughout your body,
Or the hiccups and blips in your notes.
The 'I've got this, I don't need anyone,'
Or 'I need a hug, but I'm too afraid to ask.'
The 'it's fine',
Or 'you've actually really hurt me.'
The happy posts and snapchats,
Or the sad code of your heart.
The stamp that says check,
Or the emptiness with no 'where to.'
The passionate roar of a lion,
Or the learner driver at traffic lights.
The drive and power in Schumacher,
Or the turned over car on the roundabout.
Whatever your story, it's okay,
Open your heart to someone,
You'll feel much better, that I promise.
There's a beautiful, yet broken world out there,
And I hate for you to miss out.

## Sometimes

Sometimes our toughest battles
Are completely unknown
To even those closest to us.
Sometimes our faces
Won't let them show
No matter how much they worry us.
Sometimes our greatest strength
Comes from these mysterious truths,
And that I believe is a heaven-sent gift.

## Don't

Have you ever glanced at someone
Who seems as though they could have
No problems?
Young,
Pretty,
Talented,
Intelligent,
Loved.
Don't let this fool you,
Often, it's not a situation
Or a circumstance,
It's a battle with our minds,
And that I believe is one of the toughest
Fights we will ever have to get into the ring for.
Solutions can be provided for a situation,
But your mind needs more than a clear plan.
There are no quick fixes.
It takes time.
It takes effort.
It takes commitment.
So, don't judge someone else's life
With the impression that they have no burdens
Because believe me, they do.
Not everyone's battles are displayed on their
Television screen, you may have to press red,
And buttons more to navigate your way.

## Destroyer and Reviver

You mislead me with the beauty of falling leaves-
The wonderful joy of crunching them
Refills my childhood soul inside,
But then nature does it again...
It throws the curve ball of winter.
Oh, the overwhelming frost builds within me,
And I can't escape or hibernate
Like some animals choose to do.
I have to face it now, ALONE-
Winter was so fun when I was young;
Oh, how grandpa and I had great fun in the snow.
But then I discovered
A lion roar inside-
I'm not speaking about a fire of passion,
I'm speaking about fear.
Darkness smacked me, and I couldn't see any light,
Sometimes, I struggled to get through,
And I guess that's still somewhat true...
Don't get me wrong, I love Christmas,
The buzz around church certainly kick starts my heart,
The blast of Christmas tunes blaring,
The smell of turkey and ham,
The choice of granny's one or three desserts,
A Santa hat or Christmas jumper.
Volunteering to help those in need,
But why can't people understand
That's for all seasons of life?
Chocolate and sweets,
Markets and pressies,
But be careful not to forget the real meaning,
JESUS.

When the buzz of Christmas is over
I retreat within myself again,
But now I see an open door,
And oh yes, the blessings ahead.
Christmas is for childhood, adolescence,
And of course, adulthood too.
The meaning carries with us through all seasons of life.
So, I suppose Winter is not all bad,
But I sure get some attacks,
And worry thumps off each and every organ
Like the dodgem cars do.
A dreadful hopelessness contaminates my heart and mind,
'When will it end?'
I ask myself day in, day out.
However, at such a special time
We shouldn't take our eyes off the one behind it all,
The autumn leaves and the breezy trees,
Even the dreaded bitter mornings and dark days
Are symbols of his bold creation.
He told us to rest our minds and bodies,
And that's what Winter is for,
Flip why didn't I realise this before?
The one above is calling you
Because this season is yours to hold.

*Dedicated to one of my greatest inspirations, my grandpa Tom.*

## The unknown

When people say,
'I understand,'
You have to remember
That often they don't.
Only one person knows fully,
And we can't expect others to
When we aren't certain ourselves.
Every single one of us will face unique
Challenges along our paths
Which are made to strengthen and develop us
Into who we are called to be.
So, don't wish for someone else's puzzle book
Because your questions
Will be answered by the lessons you've learnt,
And your walls will be knocked down
Using the weapons you've been provided with.
When God tells you, 'fight through this,'
Listen.
Just listen.

## Fine

I feel nothing here,
Anyone else?
A child of God,
Yet no fire within,
What on earth is the matter?
Winter is coming,
It's screaming at me already,
And I hate it.
I should be snuggled in my jammies,
But my body will not rest,
And my heart is leaping out of my chest.
I want to vomit because I am so tense,
And they say it's just in the mind,
Seriously, wise up!
I think I'm getting the cold,
But no, it's just my enemy attacking.
Anxiety is slicing up my system like it's a cake,
'What's wrong,' my family worryingly ask,
But I just don't understand,
And these days, that's my answer to most things.
A usually motivated warrior,
Now an overwhelmed worrier.
Please don't let me go back there!
The motion of my morning bus
Is sometimes all that puts me at ease
Or the comfort of crawling into bed
Knowing that once again, I can sleep.
'I'm fine,' has become my first language,
The words slipping off my tongue
Before I've even begun
I'm deceiving almost everyone,
Except myself.

## Drive on

The traffic lights will halt me,
But I know they won't be red forever.
The speed limit will slow me down,
But soon I can race on,
And they will call me Schumacher.
The bumps in the road
Will throw me around,
But soon it will be smooth again.
Whizzing round the roundabout,
Not knowing when to turn off,
But things won't be foggy for eternity.
Soon I can pass the test,
And rest at last.
I may fail,
But even that's not final.
All these signs will eventually make sense,
But for now, I will learn the road,
And try my best.
The instructor is knowledgeable,
And I will lay my trust.
I know who is really at the steering wheel,
Adding to my highlight reel.
I can't wait to celebrate,
But for now, I should concentrate,
After all, there is only so much my poor mum can take!

## We're all matches

You're the match
Connecting your light to others lives
You're the bridge
Forming life-changing friendships.
You're the spark
Igniting passion in someone else's heart.
You're the flame
In changing the world.
You're the reason
Why someone hasn't given up.
You're the paper and pen
To another human's dream.
The place the real you began
Won't be the place you will end,
But I promise you,
The lessons you've learnt will be unforgettable,
And the memories you have made
Will be treasured.
Starting points are childhood friends,
You do everything with them,
And no amount of mist will let them disappear,
But at some stage, you gotta leave them behind.
I'm not saying spiritually, but physically,
Your heart will always have a place for them.
But sometimes you have to fly,
Chase the cheetahs,
Become a starting line for someone new,
Climb the monkey bars,
And leave the limit just a little higher
Each time.
You must go because if you stay
You won't discover your 'where to?'

## What am I supposed to say?

Do I tell them I'm tired?
Then they tell me to go to bed earlier,
Switch that phone off,
That's what is keeping you awake.
NO! I want to scream,
But I don't.
I remain silent and nod in agreement
Because I know that I don't need a phone
To keep me awake-
My mind does that all on its own.
Do I tell them my health isn't good?
Then they tell me to go to the doctors,
They worry and they fret,
And they ask a question on behalf of each star in the sky,
And I can't cope with that right now.
Do I tell them I'm just feeling a bit done?
Then they panic in case I have decided
My time has come.
They rewind to the good times and won't let it go,
But they don't realise that this makes it worse,
It reminds me of my current lack of control,
And that I'm not who I used to be.
So, what am I supposed to say?
I'm depressed?
No!
I'm fine, of course
Because with that comes no questions or suggestions,
Remarks or judgements.
Instead, peace,
And that is all I could pray for at this time.

## Until

Not being able to look at my family and friends
Truthfully in the eyes,
Afraid I'll just disappoint them.
They haven't noticed
That I've drifted, I've become disconnected.
No one gets it.
No one understands.
If only people knew what was going on in my head;
Maybe they'd cut me some slack,
Maybe they'd take back those last mocking words,
Maybe they'd look at me in a different way.
You know what?
I don't mean to be lazy,
I'm just beyond unmotivated,
And I don't mean to be negative,
I'm just trapped in my own vicious thoughts.
I can't process my own feelings,
And I lose focus in less than a second,
But that doesn't mean I'm stupid.
When I push you away,
Understand that really what I mean
Is I need you,
And I can't cope with this alone.
I know you don't get it.
I know that because even I can't explain,
What's flipping going on in my brain.
Please just try to understand as best you can,
That I'm not myself right now,
And if you can,
Be patient with me
Just like I have to be with myself.
Until I recover again.

## Scars

See those marks on her skin?
They were a result of pain,
Not being understood,
From being unable to cope,
But I can tell you something...
It wasn't an act of attention,
Or for some kind of gain.
Those times were dreadful for her,
Covering her cuts with a Hollister hoodie,
And telling the world, 'I'm fine.'
She wanted to take her own life,
But one person stopped that all,
She took her to a safe place,
And never left her side just in case.
It is those kinds of friends
Who make the world a better place.
When I thought my time had come,
She urged me to see my strength,
And reminded me of my dreams.
She was lying on a hospital bed,
When I showed her my arms,
But she still reached out to me.
After all, I can't change the world
If I'm not here.

*Dedicated to Olivia Haddock.*

## If I just hold on

If I decided my time had come
How many would really care?
Would they notice the pain in my heart
Or the lost look in my eyes.
When things get so tough,
That I can't bare it,
How many people would be by my side?
One step and it could all be over
But then, would they even understand?
Probably not.
It's not the kind of hurt that I would shout
'Ouch!' if you punched me.
It's deeper than that.
I contemplated making a decision-
One that would make the pain disappear for eternity,
But if I did that, I wouldn't be here to write this poem today,
And my family would never heal.
So, if you're saying, 'If I,'
Make it a,' if I just hold on,'
And trust me, things will get better.
After all, the world is more meaningful with you here.

## Reaching out

Not many students can say their teacher helped to save their life,
But I'm one of those who can.
Even when there were cuts of rejection, hurt, anxiety,
And hopelessness all over my aching arms-
She was there for me.
I was at my lowest point,
But still, she spoke so highly of me.
I told her I couldn't do it,
She looked me in the eyes,
And said, 'Katie, yes you can, I've watched you.'
I told her I couldn't go on anymore,
And watched how her smile dropped
Which only made me more determined to stay.
Sometimes when things get so bad,
And I don't know how I'll get through the day,
I go and stand at her door,
Staring blankly with panic and uncertainty,
And miraculously, every time, she knows exactly what to do.
No matter what is going on in her own life,
She gives up her time when I need her most.
But one thing that I can't get over is that she doesn't realise
How powerful, inspirational and encouraging she truly is.


She has been the spark of hope,
And light that I most certainly needed,
And the bridge of support to reaching my dreams.
Recovery hasn't been easy, but she has helped to make it possible.
So, Mrs McMillan, thank you for everything you have done for me,
Nothing will ever make you realise how much it means to me.

*Dedicated to my incredibly inspirational Politics teacher,*
*Mrs. Jenny McMillan.*

**I'm not giving up**

People think I'm being dramatic when I say it's
A fight. But I'm not.
It's a fight within,
And please trust me when I say I need to win.
If I don't, I'll fall, I'll keep on falling,
And I'll sink.
But I don't think I'd get back up this time.
Or would I?
Everyone is around, comforting me,
Reassuring me, loving me like they always have,
But somehow, it's harder to see them all right now.
The greatest hug fails to break down
The seemingly indestructible barriers I've constructed.
So, what do I do?
I don't know currently,
But what I do know is...
I can't give up.
I've thought about it. But I won't.
No matter how hard it gets, it won't be like before
Because I've got God now,
And because of that, it's going to be okay.
So, let the anxiety flow,
And let the depression come like a brick in the face
Because I'm not giving up.

34323561R00020

Printed in Poland
by Amazon Fulfillment
Poland Sp. z o.o., Wrocław